PEACE
A DEVOTIONAL

**FINDING PEACE
IN THE MIDST OF YOUR
VALLEY EXPERIENCES:**

"HOW TO MAINTAIN YOUR PEACE"

PEACE
A DEVOTIONAL

**FINDING PEACE
IN THE MIDST OF YOUR
VALLEY EXPERIENCES:**

"HOW TO MAINTAIN YOUR PEACE"

by Minister Yvonne Carr

'N Gratitude Publishing
Aquarian Age Books

Address: 141 Lee Road # 817, Auburn, Alabama 36832
Email: : carry19573@gmail.com

Published in the United States

by 'N Gratitude Publishing Company

Atlanta Georgia

www.NGratitude.net

2016

Note: All scripture quotations are taken from the New King James Version and the New Scofield Study Bible.

The text underneath the scriptures are paraphrases.

Dedicated in the Memory Of:

Mrs. Susie Kate Pollard

Mr. George Washington Pollard

Ms. Lisa Michelle Pollard

Ms. Lola Mae Fuller

Mr. Willie Henry Carr

Mrs. Dianne Eiland

And all my love ones who have gone on
to be with the Lord!

Acknowledgements

First of all, I would like to acknowledge my God, who said, "Trust in the Lord with all of your heart; And lean not to your own understanding; in all your ways acknowledge him and he shall direct thy path." – *Proverbs 3:5-6:*

Special thanks to my husband, Donald L. Carr and to my children and grand-children: Dexter, Asami, Dexter Jr., and Hiroshi William Carr; Derrick, Donna (Carr), Derrick Jr.; and Caria Shekinah Maddox, JarMarius, April (Carr), Ashley and JarMarius Oliver, Jr. To my daughter in the Ministry, Pastor Vernita Russell Taylor and to my earthly family and friends. To Pastor Auzzie & Co-pastor Cheryl Comer, New Life Christian Center Church; to Pastor Randy and Dawn Cowart, the City Church; and to ALL the Saints who have encouraged me on this journey.

Because truly, this has been a journey,

FORWARD

One of the most amazing statements Jesus made to the body of Christ before he ascended into heaven was when he said, my Peace I give to you, not as the world giveth, give I unto you. Throughout our city, country, and the world, we find that people from all nations are in the pursuit of peace. For without it there can be no unity, freedom or rest. The peace which God gives us assures us with comfort, happiness and tranquility. That is why I believe this book will bring us to a place where we can enjoy a healthy fulfilled life that was designed for us to live everyday, abiding in this peace.

Minister Yvonne Carr has captured the essence of this peace, and put it in this book that it will bring strength and hope to tremendously bless and empower you. She, through the power of the Holy Spirit and the word of God, is presenting to you practical guidance that will help you step into your peace.

Life is short considering, the time we spend here on earth, and that is why it is important that you read this book. It will empower your ability to see and experience a greater dimension of life.

Pastor Auzzie Comer
New Life Christian Center
Opelika, Alabama

Introduction

First and foremost, I would like to give thanks to God through Jesus Christ for being my **peace** in the midst of my valley experiences and not for only being my **peace**, but for allowing me to maintain my **peace**.

Now, let us be real: While traveling life's road, you will encounter obstacles where you really will need the **peace** of God on your journey. Jesus said, in John 16:33: *"These things I have spoken unto you, that in me you might have <u>peace</u>, but in the world you shall have tribulations. But be of good cheer; I have overcome the world."*

Have you ever found yourself in a low (valley) state? It is like being trapped between mountains and a river. It feels as if the pressure and the weight of the world are suffocating you. Just as Moses and the children of Israel found themselves trapped between Pharaoh and the Red Sea, and God delivered them and gave them <u>peace</u>; God can and will deliver you and give you <u>peace</u>. He will give you <u>peace</u> of mind.

This devotional of ***<u>Peace</u> - Finding Peace in the Midst of Your Valley Experiences: How to Maintain Your Peace,*** is a book of hope in times of despair. I pray that it will be a blessing to you as you find the very presence of God. For those of you, who have for so long desired the peace of God, be assured that these scriptures will bless your spirit, body and soul.

Definitions

Peace - Absence of <u>inner</u> of <u>outer</u> conflict, unity, wholeness. Freedom from disturbance or agitation, calm; repose; a state of quiet or tranquility.
The Hebrew (Shalom) greeting that meant both the absence of conflict and God's highest blessing.
(Holman Student Bible Dictionary)

Midst – The middle position or part; Center; The condition of being surrounded by or beset by something.

A time period about the middle of a continuing condition or act; Among.
(Webster's II New College Dictionary)

Valley - A low tract of land between hills; a river-basin. An elongated low land between mountain ranges, hills, or other uplands, often having a river or stream running along the bottom.
(Webster)

Experience(s) – Apprehension or perception of an object, thought, emotion, or event through the sense or mind. To participate in personally; undergo.
(Webster's II New College Dictionary)

Definitions Continued

Maintain – Sustain, to continue, carry on, to preserve or keep in a given existing condition.
(Webster's II New College Dictionary)

Sustain – Maintain, to hold up; To keep in existence; To provide with nourishment or sustenance; To support from below; To support the spirits, vitality, or resolution of; To endure or withstand; To affirm.
(Webster's II New College Dictionary)

God's Divine and Holy Scriptures

The way to maintain your **peace** is by the word of God, through Jesus Christ with the anointing of the Holy Spirit. As you meditate and study these scriptures, let the presence of God fill your spirit, heart, mind, and soul with his **peace.**

Leviticus 26:6 - "And I will give peace in the land, and ye shall lie down, and none shall make you afraid; and I will rid evil beasts out of the land, neither shall the sword go through your land."

It is good news to know that God will give you peace in the land. God will not only give peace in the land, and in our physical bodies, but peace in our spiritual bodies as well. Also, God will cause your enemies (evil beasts) to flee from you.

Luke 1:79 - To give light to them that sit in darkness and in the shadow of death, to guide our feet into the way of peace.

Jesus is that light who was sent by God to save us from our sins and direct our feet into the way of peace.

Psalms 119:165 - Great <u>peace</u> have they who love thy law, and nothing shall offend them.

Much peace to those who love and keep the word of God.

Psalms 4:8 - I will both lie down in <u>peace</u>, and sleep; for thou, Lord, only makest me dwell in safety.

God will give you sweet peace and rest while you sleep and he will protect you from your enemies.

Isaiah 26:3 - Thou wilt keep him in perfect <u>peace</u>, whose mind is stayed on thee, because he trusteth in thee.

When we keep our mind stayed on Jesus, and totally depend, lean and trust in God, he will keep you in perfect peace.

Psalms 122:6-7 - Pray for the <u>peace</u> of Jerusalem; they shall prosper who love thee. <u>Peace</u> be within thy walls, and prosperity within thy palaces.

We should never cease from praying for peace for all nations, and God will give peace and prosperity.

I Samuel 7:14 - And the cities which the Philistines had taken from Israel were restored to Israel, from Ekron even unto Gath; and their borders did Israel deliver out of the hands of the Philistines. And there was <u>peace</u> between Israel and the Amorites.

Only God can restore peace. God will make your enemies be at peace with you.

Isaiah 9:6-7 - For unto us a child is born, unto us a son is given, and the government shall be upon his shoulder; and his name shall be called Wonderful, Counselor, The Mighty God, The Everlasting Father, The Prince of <u>Peace</u>. Of the increase of his government and <u>peace</u> there shall be no end, upon the throne of David, and upon his kingdom, to order it, and to establish it with justice and with righteousness from henceforth even forever. The zeal of the Lord of hosts will perform this.

It is a blessing to know that Jesus was born and is the Prince of Peace forever, and will always be.

Luke 2:14 - Glory to God in the highest, and on earth <u>peace</u>, good will toward men.

We know that all honor and praises belong to God. When we honor and praise him, we will have peace within.

Matthew 5:9 - Blessed are the <u>peace</u> makers; for they shall be called the children (sons) of God.

We as the saints are the peace makers and are called the children (sons) of God.

John 14:27 - <u>Peace</u> I leave with you, my <u>peace</u> I give unto you; not as the world giveth, give I unto you. Let not your heart be troubled, neither let it be afraid.

There is comfort and assurance in knowing that we have the peace of God and his protection.

Romans 5:1 - Therefore, being justified by faith, we have <u>peace</u> with God through our Lord Jesus Christ.

As saints of God, we can rest assure that we have peace through Jesus Christ.

Isaiah 53:3 - He was wounded for our transgressions, he was bruised for our iniquities; the chastisement of our <u>peace</u> was upon him, and with his stripes we are healed.

We have peace because of the punishment that Jesus took. Also, the peace of God pardon and forgives sin and brings healing.

Luke 24:36 - And as they thus spoke, Jesus himself stood in the midst of them, and saith unto them, <u>Peace</u> be unto you.

The Holy Spirit now being in you will and can speak peace into our lives.

In the following scriptures, we, as saints of God, can speak peace to one another.

I Corinthians 1:3 - Grace be unto you, and <u>peace</u>, from God, our Father, and from the Lord Jesus Christ.

I Thessalonians 1:1 - Paul, and Silvanus, and Timothy, unto the church of the Thessalonians which is in God, the Father, and in the Lord Jesus Christ: Grace be unto you, and <u>peace</u>, from God, our Father, and the Lord Jesus Christ.

II Thessalonians 1:2 - Grace unto you, and <u>peace</u>, from God the Father, and from our Lord Jesus Christ.

Romans 1:7 - To all that be in Rome, beloved of God, called to be saints: Grace to you and <u>peace</u> from God our Father, and the Lord Jesus Christ.

Galatians 1:3 - Grace be to you, and <u>peace</u>, from God the Father, and from our Lord Jesus Christ.

God's amazing grace will give you peace. Only true peace comes from God.

Revelation 1:4 - John to the seven churches which are in Asia: Grace be unto you, and <u>peace</u> from him which is, and which was, and which is to come; and from the seven spirits which are before his throne.

Peace comes from the Alpha and Omega (God).

Philippians 4:7 - And the <u>peace</u> of God, which passeth all understanding, shall keep your hearts and minds through Christ Jesus.

There is no other peace like the peace of God, who is able to keep you from having heart attacks and from losing your mind.

Jeremiah 29:7 - And seek the <u>peace</u> of the city whither I have caused you to be carried away captives, and pray unto the Lord for it: for in the <u>peace</u> thereof shall ye have <u>peace</u>.

God will give you peace when you pray, seek, pursue, run and go after it no matter where you are and what the circumstances may be.

I Kings 2:33 - Their blood shall therefore return upon the head of Joab, and upon the head of his seed forever; but upon David, and upon his seed, and upon his house, and upon his throne, shall there be <u>peace</u> forever from the Lord.

The Children of God and their seed will always have peace.

Numbers 6:26 - "The Lord lift up his countenance upon thee and give thee <u>peace</u>.

May the presence of God shine his peace upon you.

Proverbs 16:7 - When a man's ways please the Lord, he maketh even his enemies to be at <u>peace</u> with him.

When you obey God's word and do what is pleasing in His sight, He will cause your enemies to be at peace with you.

Isaiah 45:7 - I form the light, and create darkness: I make <u>peace</u>, and create evil: I the Lord do all these things.

Only real peace comes from God.

Jeremiah 14:13 - Then said I, Ah Lord God! Behold, the prophets say unto them, ye shall not see the sword, neither shall ye have famine; but I will give you assured <u>peace</u> in this place.

Trouble nor lack shall come near you, this is the assurance of the peace of God.

Psalms 34:14 - Depart from evil, and do good; seek <u>peace</u>, and pursue it.

Search and seek for the peace of God, go after it. Lay hold on it.

Ephesians 2:13-14 - But now in Christ Jesus ye who sometimes far off are made nigh by the blood of Christ. For he is our <u>peace</u>, who hath made both one, and hath broken down the middle wall of partition between us.

Thank God for the blood of Jesus who is our Peace and who has brought us back into unity in oneness with Him.

Romans 16:20 - And the God of <u>peace</u> shall bruise Satan under your feet shortly. The grace of our Lord Jesus Christ be with you. Amen.

We serve notice to you Satan, that the peace of God is all powerful and nothing can withstand Him.

Isaiah 26:12 - Lord, thou wilt ordain <u>peace</u> for us: for thou also hast wrought all our works in us.

The peace of God has been ordained for you and work in you by the Holy Spirit.

Philippians 4:9 - Those things, which ye have both learned, and received, and heard, and seen in me, do: and the God of <u>peace</u> shall be with you.

The wisdom of God brings peace. Hold fast and receive, do and live the word of God so that you shall obtain peace.

Romans 14:19 - Let us therefore follow after the things which make for <u>peace</u>, and things wherewith one may edify another.

Follow after righteousness and holiness that you may obtain peace and encourage one another.

I Corinthians 7:15 - But if the unbelieving depart, let him depart. A brother or a sister is not under bondage in such cases: but God hath called us to <u>peace</u>.

When others walk away, you hold on to God's peace.

Ephesians 4:3 - Endeavoring to keep the unity of the Spirit in the bond of peace.

The peace of God brings oneness.

I Thessalonians 5:13 - And to esteem them very highly in love for their work's sake. And be at peace, with them that call on the Lord out of a pure heart.

Maintain and keep peace with the Saints.

II Timothy 2:22 - Flee also youthful lusts: but follow righteousness, faith, charity, peace, with them that call on the Lord out of a pure heart.

Turn from your evil ways and follow godliness, hope, love and peace with the saints.

James 3:18 - And the fruit of righteousness is sown in peace of them that make peace.

Righteousness bares peace.

I Peter 3:11 - Let him eschew evil, and do good; let him seek peace, and ensue it.

Turn from evil and search diligently for the peace of God, capture and seize it.

Acts 10:36 - The word which God sent unto the children of Israel, preaching <u>peace</u> by Jesus Christ: (he is Lord of all).

Jesus was sent by God to preach peace to everyone. Jesus is the prince of peace.

Romans 8:6 - For to be carnally minded is death; but to be spiritually minded is life and <u>peace</u>.

We have the peace of God only when we are spiritually minded.

Colossians 3:15 - And let the <u>peace</u> of God rule in your hearts, to the also ye are called in one body; and be ye thankful.

Saints, let the peace of God reign and have control of your hearts and give God the praise.

I Thessalonians 5:23 - And the very God of <u>peace</u> sanctify you wholly; and I pray God your whole spirit and soul and body be preserved blameless unto the coming of our Lord Jesus Christ.

The peace of God will cleanse and set you apart that no fault will be found in you when Jesus returns.

II Thessalonians 3:16 - Now the Lord of peace himself give you peace always by all means. The Lord will be with you.

The peace of God will be with you always.

Psalms 29:11 - The Lord will give strength unto his people; the Lord will bless his people with peace.

Strength and peace belongs to God, who will give it to his people.

Psalms 85:8 - I will hear what God the Lord will speak: for he will speak peace unto his people, and to his saints: but let them not turn again to folly.

Saints hear and receive the peace of God, so that you will not fall into sin again.

Galatians 6:16 - And as many as walk according to this rule, peace be on them, and mercy, and upon the Israel of God.

When we walk accordingly, and be obedient to the commandments of God, we will have peace and mercy.

Ephesians 6:23 - <u>Peace</u> be to the brethren, and love with faith, from God the Father and the Lord Jesus Christ.

God will give peace to all the saints.

Luke 2:13-14 - And suddenly there was with the angel a multitude of the heavenly host praising God, and saying, Glory to God in the highest, and on earth <u>peace</u>, good will toward men.

Let all the saints give praises unto the Lord of peace.

Luke 19:37-38 - And when he was come nigh, even now at the descent of the mount of olives, the whole multitude of the disciples began to rejoice and praise God with a loud voice for all the mighty works they had seen; Saying Blessed be the King that cometh in the name of Lord: <u>peace</u> in heaven, and glory in the highest.

Let all the saints rejoice and praise the King of peace.

Psalms 91:1 - He who dwelleth in the secret place of the Most High shall abide under the shadow of the Almighty.

It is good to know that you can find peace beneath the wings/shadow of an almighty God when you stay or remain in that secret place. Know that God has you covered through Christ Jesus.

A Message from the Author

I thank God, who has allowed me the honor and privilege of writing this devotional pertaining to Godly peace, under the inspiration of the Holy Spirit. Writing it has been an encouragement to me, and I hope it will inspire you to do what God has called you to do. I know that God has a plan for each one of us, but we must find out what His Will is for our lives and pursue it.

I thank God for many years of much fasting and prayer, and allowing me, who is so unworthy, to be instilled with his wisdom, knowledge and understanding in my spirit. Again, I am so ever grateful and thankful for what God is doing in my life and in the lives of the saints.

The peace of God has always been in our midst, but it has been up to us to search, seek and pursue it. I leave you with this thought: know that your faith in God is all you need to move forward. May God bless and keep you is my prayer.

Biography

A child of the most High God, who gives Him all the praise, honor and glory for saving her and filling her with the Holy Ghost, and being a servant for HIM; Reverend Yvonne Carr accepted her calling as a Minister in 1997. Since then, she has continued to do the Will of God. She received her Certificate of License on July 20, 1997 and her Certificate of Ordination, May 2, 2004.

Reverend Carr is the the wife of Donald L. Carr, a mother of three and the grand-mother of six. She is affiliated with The City Church in Auburn, Alabama, Pastor Randy and First Lady Dawn Cowart.

Minister Carr is currently employed as an Administrative Assistant at Tuskegee University, in the Office of Student Life and Development/Student Government Association. She received an Associate Degree in Science from Southern Union State Community College, Wadley, AL, on December 12, 2011.

She enjoys writing poetry and songs and published her first poem in "2001," in the book entitled: "What Tomorrow Holds."

To God Be All the Glory, Honor and Praise!

AEP

ACCEPT - ENDURE – PATIENCE

**Lord help me to Accept
the things I cannot change
Give me the strength to Endure
the things I have to
And Patience to wait on you**

Peace and blessings,
Yvonne Carr

Notes:

Notes: